FREIGHTMASTER

PUBLISHING

Compilation, Design & Research : Martin Buck

Fleet Lists & Research : Mark Rawlinson

ISBN : 978-0-9558275-2-5

Published by :
Freightmaster Publishing
158 Overbrook
SWINDON
SN3 6AY

www.freightmasterpublishing.co.uk

01793 - 644957

Printed by :
Stephens & George Ltd
Goat Mill Road
MERTHYR TYDFIL
CF48 3TD

www.stephensandgeorge.co.uk

01685 - 388888

December 2009

INTRODUCTION

Welcome, to Wagon Recognition - Volume 2, the follow up to our successful Volume 1, published in April 2008 featuring Carkinds BAA to WIA inclusive.

Volume 2 covers:

- Departmental Wagons.
- On Track Plant (OTP).

which have a TOPS Carkind prefix of 'Y' and 'Z', respectively.

As with the previous volume, all Carkinds are fully illustrated and this time we have added more information about each one, by including:

- 'Design' code.
- operating 'Pool' code.

This book is not intended for 'number' crunchers, but will be a valuable identification aid for enthusiasts, modellers and railway professionals alike. It has been more difficult to compile than Volume 1 because some OTP machines are:

- unrecorded on TOPS when it comes to their movements.
- transported to engineers possession by road or do not move around the network under their own power, which makes it more difficult to track them down.
- used by their operators (ie, Balfour Beatty, Jarvis, etc.) in Europe and may have extended periods of absence away from the UK rail network.

However, to the best of our knowledge and having undertaken painstaking research, this volume is complete and represents an accurate picture of the wagons and OTP currently in use at the time of publication. If there are any omissions, this is regrettable and we offer our apologies in advance, but this should not detract from what this book sets out to achieve.

Finally, I would like to thank all the people who have helped during compilation and to those who have kindly contributed images, without which this publication would not be possible. There are too many people to thank individually, but I must extend my thanks and appreciation in particular to Gareth Bayer, whose assistance has been immense.

Now, please enjoy Wagon Recognition : Volume 2.

Martin Buck
December 2009

Opposite :

ZWA - B : Plasser & Theurer 08-4x4 / 4S-RT Tamper
No. : DR 73905
Location : Westbury
(Martin Buck)

CONTENTS

INTRODUCTION 3

OVERVIEW 6

LEGEND 7

'Y' CARKINDS

YDA	Ballast & Spoil Handling Trains	8
YEA	Welded Rail Carriers	17
YFA	'Slingers'	22
YGA	Ballast Hopper Wagons	27
YJA	Track Renewal Trains	31
YJB	Cranes	34
YKA	Rail & Sleeper Carriers	40
YLA	Rail & Sleeper Carriers	40
YOA	Ballast & Spoil Handling Trains	41
YOB	Cranes	44
YQA	Rail & Sleeper Carriers	45
YSA	Rail & Sleeper Carriers	46
YSA	Track Renewal Support Vehicles	47
YWA	Rail & Sleeper Carriers	50
YXA	Rail & Sleeper Carriers	52
YXA	Track Renewal Support Vehicles	54
YXA	Multi Purpose Vehicles (MPVs)	57
YZA	Stoneblowers	60

'Z' CARKINDS

ZAA	2-Axle Open Wagon	62
ZCA	2-Axle Open Wagon	63
ZIA / ZIB	Cranes	67
ZOA	Cranes	70
ZUA	Brake Vans	75
ZWA	Track Machines	
	Dynamic Track Stabilisers	78
	Tampers	79
	Ballast Cleaners	104
	Ballast Regulators	109
ZWA	Rail Grinders	112
ZWA	General Maintenance Vehicles - TRAMMS	118
ZWA	Snowblower	122
ZWB	Track Machines - Ballast Cleaners	123
ZWQ	Track Machines - Tampers	124
ZWY	Track Machines - Tampers	124
ZXQ	Research Vehicles	126
ZZA	Snowploughs	127

GLOSSARY

Carkinds Removed	130
On Track Plant (OTP) - Explained	138
Wagons & OTP Pool Codes	142
Bibliography	144

OVERVIEW

TOPS CODES

TOPS (Total Operating Processing System) manages the movement of locomotives, rolling stock and track machines. Accordingly, whilst each vehicle has a unique number, each type is classified by way of a ***three letter*** coding, called a ***'Carkind'***, where for this volume:

The **First Letter** identifies the wagon / vehicle category.

Y	Bogie Departmental Wagons / Track Machines
Z	2-Axle Departmental Wagons / Track Machines

The **Second Letter** identifies the Type - size / capacity, etc.

The **Third Letter** identifies the brake type:

A	Air Brake
B	Air Brake, through vacuum pipe
O	No Brake, unfitted
P	No Brake, with vacuum through pipe
Q	No Brake, with air through pipe
R	No Brake, air and vacuum through pipe
V	Vacuum Brake
W	Vacuum Brake with air through pipe
X	Dual Brake, air and vacuum
Y	Unfitted - vehicle cannot be train consisted

'D' PREFIX

Engineers wagons are numbered with a '**D**' prefix followed by a second letter, 'B' or 'C'.

On Track Plant is prefixed '**DR'** (Reportable to TOPS or '**DX'** (Not reportable to TOPS).

Some vehicles have a letter after the 'DR' prefix, which indicates the manufacturer.

ABOUT THIS BOOK

Firstly, this book ***does not*** include:

- complete lists of numbers for Wagons and OTP vehicles.
- technical measurements.
- OTP which do not have a three-letter Carkind reference.
- departmental coaching stock.
- road / rail plant vehicles.
- small plant.

However, it ***does*** include for each Carkind:

- Wagon types and OTP vehicles in use on the rail network.
- a photograph for each Wagon and OTP listed.
- details of the number range for each listing.
- 'Design' & Operating 'Pool' codes.

During compilation, several Carkinds were 'In Store' or withdrawn and, whilst excluded from the main part of the book, some examples are recorded in the Glossary for completeness.

LEGEND

For each 'Carkind' listed, the following details are given:

1. 3-Letter 'Carkind' reference + suffix.
2. Title.
3. 'Active' Number Range in which the wagon(s) will be listed.
4. Notes (where applicable) of any important details, such as conversions, etc.

Example:

YDA - C	**Skako Ballast Distribution Train Hopper - 'Octopus'**
Number Range	
DR 92213 - DR 92222	
Design Code	
YD003A	
Operating 'Pool'	
6107	
Notes	
Built in 1982 by Standard Wagon and converted by Powell Duffryn.	

Each separate Carkind listing is backed up by an illustration to show the design and any associated livery(s), plus an informative caption providing details of the:

- Carkind reference
- Vehicle number
- Location of illustration
- Manufacturer(s) details
- Photograph accreditation

Abbreviations:

DBS	:	DB Schenker
EWS	:	English, Welsh & Scottish Railways (now DB Schenker)
NR	:	Network Rail
P & T	:	Plasser & Theurer

NOTES :

1. The Y's are listed alphabetically in 4-letter Carkind sequence.
2. The Z's are listed by 3-letter Carkind, in ascending number range sequence.
3. A photograph is included for each separate Carkind, but please note that some OTP vehicles have different 'ends', but only one image is included.
4. References to GrantPlant should be taken to read VolkerRail.

YDA - C — Skako Ballast Distribution Train Hopper - 'Octopus'

Number Range DR 92213 - DR 92222

Design Code YD003A

Operating 'Pool' 6107

Notes Built in 1982 by Standard Wagon and converted by Powell Duffryn. Owned by DB Schenker.

YDA - D — P & T (NFS-D) Ballast Distribution Train Hopper

Number Range DR 92223 - DR 92240

Design Code YD004A

Operating 'Pool' 8852

Notes Owned by Network Rail.

YDA - E — P & T (MFS-D) Ballast Distribution Train Hopper

Number Range	Design Code	Operating 'Pool'
DR 92241 - DR 92254	YD005A	8854
DR 92265 - DR 92279	YD005B	8858
DR 92295 - DR 92330	YD005D	8860
DR 92341 - DR 92346	YD005D	8860

Notes

Owned by Network Rail.

YDA - E — P & T Seco-Rail RM90-NR Rail Ballast Cleaner Hopper

Number Range DR 92377

Design Code YD005E

Operating 'Pool' 7370

Notes Distinctive black, orange & yellow livery. Runs with DR 92400 + DR 76601. Owned by Colas Rail.

YDA - E P & T (MFS-D) Ballast Distribution Train Hopper

Number Range DR 92441 - DR 92476

Design Code YD005F

Operating 'Pool' 8854 8858 8860

Notes Owned by Network Rail.

YDA - F P & T (MFS-SB) Swivel Conveyor Hopper

Number Range	Design Code	Operating 'Pool'
DR 92259 - DR 92262	YD006A	8854
DR 92280 - DR 92281	YD006B	8858
DR 92287 - DR 92294	YD006D	8860
DR 92333 - DR 92340	YD006D	8860

Notes

Owned by Network Rail - runs with DR 92400 + DR 76601.

YDA - G P & T (MFS-A) Medium Output Ballast Cleaner, Interface Wagon

Number Range DR 92282 - DR 92283

Design Code YD007A

Operating 'Pool' 8858

Notes Owned by Network Rail.

YDA - G P & T Seco-Rail (MFS-A) Ballast Cleaner, Interface Wagon

Number Range DR 92400

Design Code YD007B

Operating 'Pool' 7370

Notes Distinctive black / orange / yellow livery.

Runs with DR 92377 + DR 76601.

Owned by Colas Rail.

YDA - C
No. DR 92219
Built : See text
Location : Didcot Yard
(Brian Daniels)

YDA - C
No. DR 92221
Built : See text
Location : Didcot Yard
(Brian Daniels)

YDA - D	**Built**	**: 2000 by Plasser & Theurer**
No. DR 92231	**Location**	**: Doncaster station**
	(Mark Franklin)	

YDA - E	**Built**	**: 2000 by Plasser & Theurer**
No. DR 92241	**Location**	**: Peterborough**
	(Gareth Bayer)	

YDA - E — Built : 2000 by Plasser & Theurer
No. DR 92242 — Location : Peterborough
(Gareth Bayer)

YDA - E — Built : 2009 by Plasser & Theurer
No. DR 92473 — Location : Warrington, Arpley
(Stuart Daniels)

YDA - F | **Built : 2000 - 2005 by Plasser & Theurer**
No. DR 92291 | **Location : Didcot Avoiding Line**
(Martyn Read)

YDA - G | **Built : 2000 by Plasser & Theurer**
No. DR 92283 | **Location : Carlisle Citadel**
(Nathan Williamson)

YDA - E Built : 2006 by Plasser & Theurer
No. DR 92377 Location : Eastleigh Works *(Gareth Bayer)*

YDA - G Built : 2006 by Plasser & Theurer
No. DR 92400 Location : Eastleigh Works *(Gareth Bayer)*

YEA - A	Built	: 1985 by BREL Doncaster
No. 979133	Location	: Peterborough
	(Gareth Bayer)	

YEA - A	Built	: 1985 by BREL Doncaster
No. 979412	Location	: Clapham Junction
	(Martyn Read)	

YEA - A — Continuous Welded Rail Wagon - 'Perch'

Number Range 979001 - 979134

Design Code YE007C YE007D YE007E

Operating 'Pool' 8812

Notes The illustration for this wagon type shows ex-'Railtrack' green livery.

YEA - A — Continuous Welded Rail 'Clamping' Wagon - 'Perch'

Number Range 979409 979412 979415

Design Code YE010C YE010D YE010E

Operating 'Pool' 8812

YEA - A — Continuous Welded Rail 'Gantry' Wagon - 'Perch'

Number Range 979604 979607 979609
979611 - 979614

Design Code YE009A YE009C

Operating 'Pool' 8810

YEA - B — Continuous Welded Rail 'End Train' Wagon - 'Porpoise'

Number Range 979504 - 979515

Design Code YE006A YE006C

Operating 'Pool' 8810 8812 8814

YEA - D — Cowans Sheldon Continuous Welded Rail 'Chute' Wagon 'Porpoise'

Number Range NLU 979500 - NLU 979503 NLU 979507 NLU 979508
NLU 979510 NLU 979512

Design Code YE006A YE006B

Operating 'Pool' 8832

Equipment / Module Notes:

YEA - A to YEA - B 979604 - 979515

Wagons in these number ranges have modules mounted on the 'flats', which are numbered thus:

Module Nos.	Mounted On
DR 89104 - DR 89107 & DR 89109	DB 979604 - DB 979607 & DB 979609
DR 89111 - DR 89114	DB 979611 - DB 979614
DR 89204 - DR 89209	DB 979504 - DB 979509
DR 89211 - DR 89215	DB 979511 - DB 979515

YEA - A	**Built**	**: 1985 by BREL Doncaster**
No. 979609	**Location**	**: Didcot**
	(Gareth Bayer)	

YEA - A	**Built**	**: 1985 by BREL Doncaster**
No. 979611	**Location**	**: Eastleigh**
	(Martyn Read)	

YEA - B	Built	: 1985 by BREL Crewe
No. 979504	Location	: Peterborough
	(Gareth Bayer)	

YEA - B	Built	: 1985 by BREL Doncaster
No. 979511	Location	: Eastleigh
	(Martyn Read)	

YEA - D
No. 979502

Built : 1983 - 1985 by BREL, Shildon / Crewe
Location : Peterborough *(Gareth Bayer)*

YEA - D Built : 1983 - 1985 by BREL, Shildon / Crewe
No. 979503 Location : Whitemoor, March *(Gareth Bayer)*

YFA - E

Jarvis 'Slinger' Wagon

Number Range	DR 92564 - DR 92571
Design Code	YF015N
Operating 'Pool'	958
Notes	Built 1987 - 1988 by Arbel Fauvet, France. Converted in 2004 by Jarvis, York.

YFA - F

Jarvis Rail Recovery Train, Twin Jib 'Slinger' Wagon

Number Range	DR 92507 - DR 92512
Design Code	YF015B YF015C YF015H
Operating 'Pool'	958
Notes	Built 1987 - 1988 by Arbel Fauvet, France. Converted in 2001 by Jarvis, York. Not to be confused with KFA wagons in the 92500 - 92542 number range.

YFA - G

Jarvis Rail Recovery Train, Single Jib 'Slinger' Wagon

Number Range	DR 92513 - DR 92518
Design Code	YF015E YF015F YF015J
Operating 'Pool'	958
Notes	Built 1987 - 1988 by Arbel Fauvet, France. Converted 2001 - 2004 by Jarvis, York. Not to be confused with KFA wagons in the 92500 - 92542 number range.

YFA - H

Jarvis Sleeper Delivery Train, 'Slinger' Wagon

Number Range	DR 92519 - DR 92561
Design Code	YF015G YF015K YF015L YF015M
Operating 'Pool'	958
Notes	Built 1987 - 1988 by Arbel Fauvet, France. Converted 2001 - 2004 by Jarvis, York. Not to be confused with KFA wagons in the 92500 - 92542 number range.

YFA - G	Built	: See text
No. DR 92513	Location	: Didcot Yard

(Gareth Bayer)

YFA - E	Built	: See text
No. DR 92568	Location	: Water Orton

(Mark Franklin)

YFA - F	Built	: See text
No. DR 92509	Location	: Taunton

(Allan Wright)

YFA - H — Built : See text
No. DR 92551 — Location : Burton on Trent
(Gareth Bayer)

YFA - H — Built : See text
No. DR 92538 — Location : Rugby
(Richard A. Jones)

YGB - A
No. 982806

Built : See text
Location : Tonbridge West Yard

(Richard A. Jones)

YGA - A / YGB - A / YGB - E — EWS Bogie Ballast Hopper - 'Seacow'

Number Range

980000 - 980250

982440 - 982699

982700 - 982927

Operating 'Pool' 6280 6282

Notes Built 1971 - 1982 by BREL Ashford and Shildon.

YGB - D — EWS Bogie Ballast Hopper, with Generator - 'Stingray'

Number Range

980000 - 980250

982440 - 982699

982700 - 982927

Operating 'Pool' 6280 6282

Notes Built 1971 - 1982 by BREL Ashford and Shildon.

YGH - B / YGH - F — EWS Bogie Ballast Hopper - 'Sealion'

Number Range

982440 - 982699

982700 - 982927

Operating 'Pool' 6280 6282

Notes Built 1971 - 1982 by BREL Ashford and Shildon.

Design Codes:

Seacow

YGA - A	YG500X	YG500Y	YG500Z	
YGB - A	YG500A	YG500H	YG500K	YG500L
YGB - E	YG500Q	YG500R	YG500V	

Stingray

YGB - D	YG500H	YG500M	YG500T

Sealion

YGH - B	YG500B	YG500G
YGH - F	YG500S	

YGA - A Built : See text
No. 982867 Location : Rugby
(Martyn Read)

YGB - D Built : See text
No. 980210 Location : Peterborough
(Gareth Bayer)

YGB - E | Built : See text
No. 980210 | Location : Tonbridge West Yard
(Richard A. Jones)

YGH - B | Built : See text
No. 982740 (Miscoded) | Location : Westbury
(Martyn Read)

YGH - F
No. 982637

Built : See text
Location : Peterborough

(Gareth Bayer)

YJA - B
YJA - C
YJA - D
YJA - E

Matisa P 95 UK

Code	Number Range	Design Code	Operating 'Pool'
YJA - B	DR 78801	YJ021A	8844
YJA - C	DR 78811	YJ022A	8844
YJA - D	DR 78821	YJ023A	8844
YJA - E	DR 78831	YJ024A	8844

Notes

Built 2004 by Matisa - owned by Network Rail.

Illustrations of this train of 'many parts' are shown overleaf on pages 32 and 33, photographed during a shunting operation into the headshunt at Fairwater Yard, Taunton.

All 6 images taken by Nathan Williamson.

YJA - F

Harsco Track Technologies Self-Powered Wagon

Number Range DR 78701 DR 78702

Design Code YJ025A

Operating 'Pool' 7104

Notes Owned by Balfour Beatty.

YJA - F	**Built**	**: 2004 by Harsco Track Technologies**
No. DR 78701	**Location**	**: Totnes**
	(Nathan Williamson)	

DC 78801

DC 78811

DC 78821

DC 78821

DC 78821

DC 78831

YJB - C Cowans Sheldon Heavy Duty Twin Jib Crane

Number Range

DRC 78225 - DRC 78237

Design Code

YJ019C

Operating 'Pool'

7073 : DRC 78229 / 78237

7426 : DRC 78226

7776 : DRC 78227 / 78230 / 78234 / 78235

7880 : DRC 78225

7882 : DRC 78231

Notes

Several livery variations - owned by Balfour Beatty, Grant Rail, Jarvis, Network Rail, etc.
Not to be confused with numbers in the 78200 - 78278 range for TDA bogie petroleum tanks.

YJB - P P & T Heavy Duty Twin Jib Crane

Number Range

DRP 78211 - DRP 78224

Design Code

YJ018B YJ018D

Operating 'Pool'

7104 : DRP 78216 / 78221 / 78222 / 78223/ 78224

7222 : DRP 78219

7350 : DRP 78213

7426 : DRP 78211 / 78212 / 78215 / 78217

Notes

Several livery variations - owned by Balfour Beatty, Grant Rail, Jarvis, Network Rail, etc.
Not to be confused with numbers in the 78200 - 78278 range for TDA bogie petroleum tanks.

YJB - C
Built : 1979 - 1980 by Cowans Sheldon
No. : DRC 78232
Location : Newport
(Martyn Read)

YJB - P
Built : 1977 - 1980
by Cowans Sheldon
No. : DRP 78215
Location : Teignmouth
(Martyn Read)

YJB - P
Built : 1977 - 1980 by Plasser & Theurer
No. : DRP 78217
Location : Teignmouth
(Martyn Read)

YLA - B
Rebuilt : 1981 - 1982 by BREL Shildon
No. : 967516
Location : Otford Junction
(Richard A. Jones)

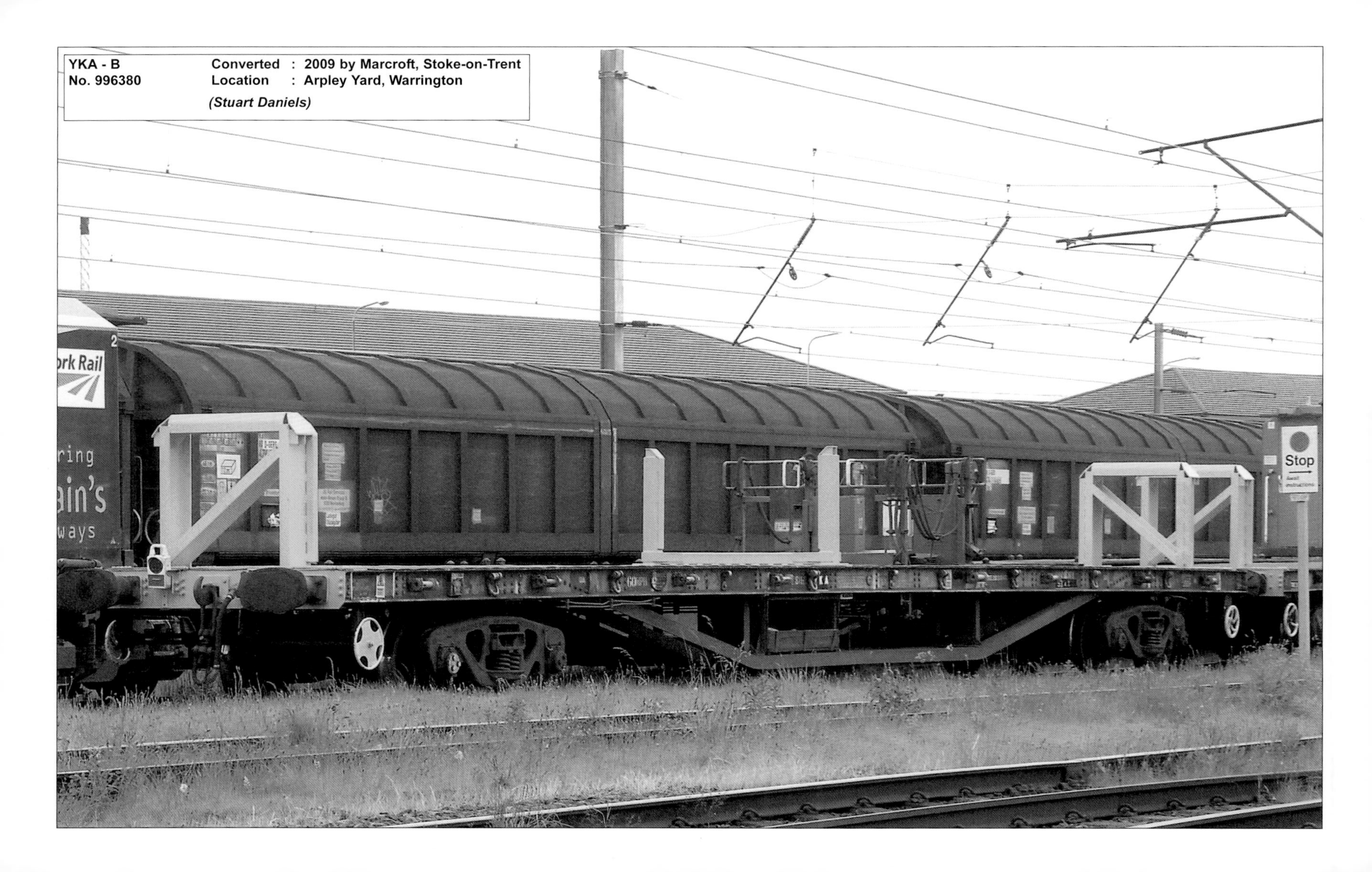

YKA - B	Converted : 2009 by Marcroft, Stoke-on-Trent
No. 996380	Location : Arpley Yard, Warrington

(Stuart Daniels)

YKA - B Borail Wagon - 'Osprey'

Number Range

996102 - 997019

Design Code

YK001A / B C / D / E / F / G / I / N / P

Operating 'Pool'

6728

Notes

Converted in 2009 from YSA and YWA wagons and fitted with stanchions, enabling 30ft and 60ft track panels to be secured in place without the need of strapping.

YKA - B Close Up of Stanchion (Stuart Daniels)

YLA - B Borail Wagon - 'Mullet'

Number Range

967501 - 967648

Design Code

YL003A

Operating 'Pool'

6820

YOA - L P & T (MFS-PW) Ballast Distribution Train, Power Wagon

Number Range

DR 92263

Design Code

YO018B

Operating 'Pool'

8854

Notes

All YOA -L wagons detailed on this page are owned by Network Rail.

YOA - L P & T (NB-PW) Ballast Distribution Train, Power Wagon

Number Range

DR 92264

Design Code

YO019A

Operating 'Pool'

8852

YOA - L P & T (MFS-A) Ballast Distribution Train, Power Wagon

Number Range

DR 92285 DR 92331

Design Code

YO018B

Operating 'Pool'

8860

YOA - L P & T (NPW-RT) Ballast Distribution Train, Power Wagon

Number Range

DR 92286 DR 92332

Design Code

YO019B

Operating 'Pool'

8860

Illustrations of each of the above carkinds are shown on page 42 and page 43.

YOA - L	Rebuilt	: 2000 by Plasser & Theurer
No. DR 92263	Location	: Carlisle Citadel station
	(Nathan Williamson)	

YOA - L	Rebuilt	: 2000 by Plasser & Theurer
No. DR 92264	Location	: Crewe Gresty Bridge
	(Gareth Bayer)	

YOA - L	Rebuilt	: 2000 - 2005 by Plasser & Theurer
No. DR 92285	Location	: Reading West Yard
	(Richard A. Jones)	

YOA - L	Rebuilt	: 2000 - 2005 by Plasser & Theurer
No. DR 92286	Location	: Westbury
	(Richard A. Jones)	

YOB - P — P & T Heavy Duty Diesel Hydraulic Crane

Number Range DRP 81504 - DRP 81532

Design Code YO010B

Operating 'Pool' 7104 7426 7882

Notes Owned by Balfour Beatty and Fastline.

YOB - P	Built	: 1978 - 1981 by Plasser & Theurer
No. DRP 81521	Location	: Peterborough *(Gareth Bayer)*

YOB - P	Built	: 1978 - 1981 by Plasser & Theurer
No. DRP 81507	Location	: Ashford *(Gareth Bayer)*

YQA - A	Borail Wagon - 'Parr'		
Number Range	967500 - 967649		
Design Code	YS043A	YSO43C	YS043D
Operating 'Pool'	6718	6720	
Notes	Numbered within YLA 'Mullet' number range.		

YQA - A	Re-built	: 1981 - 1982 by BREL, Shildon
No. 967554	Location	: Whittlesea *(Gareth Bayer)*

YQA - A	Re-built	: 1981 - 1982 by BREL, Shildon
No. 967611	Location	: Dawlish *(Anthony Christie)*

YSA - A
YSA - C

Track Panel Carrier - 'Salmon'

Number Range	996102 - 997019
Design Code	YS044A YS044C
Operating 'Pool'	6718 6720
Notes	Some wagons in the range were formerly coded YFA and YMA.

Build Details:

Number Range	Lot No.	Manufacturer
996102 - 996151	2363	1952 by Head & Wrightson
996215 - 996308	2534	1954 - 1955 by Head & Wrightson
996310 - 996361	2615	1954 - 1955 by G R Turner Ltd
996363 - 996420	2894	1956 by G R Turner Ltd
996421 - 996518	2926	1956 - 1957 by G R Turner Ltd
996519 - 996597	3065	1958 by Teeside S & E
996598 - 996670	3067	1957 - 1958 by G R Turner Ltd
996804 - 996879	3261	1959 - 1960 by BREL, Wolverton
996882 - 996921	3262	1960 by BREL, Wolverton
996923 - 996968	3284	1961 by BREL, Wolverton
996970 - 996993	3352	1962 by Powell Duffryn
996999 - 997015	3353	1960 - 1961 by Head & Wrightson

NB: The above number ranges are not 'YSA' exclusive and include some 'YWA' coded wagons as well.

YSA - A **Built : See text**
No. 996229 **Location : Dawlish Warren**
(Martyn Read)

YSA - A	**NRWH Davis 60' Flat Wagon Support Vehicle**
Number Range	979118 - 979121
Design Code	YS046A
Operating 'Pool'	8008
Notes	Owned by Network Rail.

YSA - B	**NR Support Vehicle**
Number Range	DR 92701 - DR 92706
Design Code	YS045A
Operating 'Pool'	8840
Notes	Owned by Network Rail. Works with the YJA Track Renewal Train.

YSA - B	Built	: 2004 by W H Davis
No. DR 92701	Location	: Taunton
	(Nathan Williamson)	

(Above): **YSA - C**
No. 996633
Built : See text
Location : Peterborough
(Gareth Bayer)

(Below): **YSA - A**
No. 979119
Built : 1985 by BREL Doncaster
Location : Crewe Gresty Bridge
(Gareth Bayer)

YSA
DB 979119
Network Rail

YWA - A
YWA - B
Track Panel Carrier - 'Salmon'

Number Range

996145 - 996993

Design Code

YWA - A :

YW001A / B / F / H / K

YW002A / B

YBA - B :
YW001G / J

YW003A / B / C

YW004A / B

Operating 'Pool'

6718

6720 6722

Notes

Some wagons in the range were formerly coded YFA and YMA.

Build Details:

Number Range	Lot No.	Manufacturer
996102 - 996151	2363	1952 by Head & Wrightson
996215 - 996308	2534	1954 - 1955 by Head & Wrightson
996310 - 996361	2615	1954 - 1955 by G R Turner Ltd
996363 - 996420	2894	1956 by G R Turner Ltd
996421 - 996518	2926	1956 - 1957 by G R Turner Ltd
996519 - 996597	3065	1958 by Teeside S & E
996598 - 996670	3067	1957 - 1958 by G R Turner Ltd
996804 - 996879	3261	1959 - 1960 by BREL, Wolverton
996882 - 996921	3262	1960 by BREL, Wolverton
996923 - 996968	3284	1961 by BREL, Wolverton
996970 - 996993	3352	1962 by Powell Duffryn

NB: The above number ranges are not 'YWA' exclusive, but include 'YSA' coded wagons as well.

Illustrations Opposite :

Top Right:

YWA - A	**Built**	**: See text**
No. 996595	**Location**	**: Dawlish**

Bottom Right:

YWA - B	**Built**	**: See text**
No. 996941	**Location**	**: Millbrook**

(Martyn Read - 2)

YXA - L NR Sleeper Carrier

Number Range

DR 92601 - DR 92665

Design Code

YX074A

Operating 'Pool'

8840

Notes

Owned by Network Rail.

YXA - P Continuous Welded Rail Wagon

Number Range

DR 89004 - DR 89009

Design Code

YX045A / C / D

Operating 'Pool'

8810 8812 8814

Notes

Works with YEA Continuous Welded Rail Train - number range not to be confused with TEA wagons.

YXA - P **Built : 1985 by Cowans Boyd**
No. DR 89004 **Location : Peterborough**
(Gareth Bayer)

YXA - L	Built	: 2004 by W H Davis
No. DR 92614	Location	: Fairwater Yard, Taunton
	(Martyn Read)	

YXA - L	Built	: 2004 by W H Davis
No. DR 92651	Location	: Fairwater Yard, Taunton
	(Nathan Williamson)	

YXA - D
YXA - E
YXA - F

Jarvis 'Slinger' Power Vehicle

Number Range	Design Code	
DR 92502	YX073D	YXA - D
DR 92503	YX073B	YXA - D
DR 92563	YX073G	YXA - E
DR 92520	YX073C	YXA - F
DR 92525	YX073E	YXA - F
DR 92533 - DR 92534	YX073F	YXA - F
DR 92548 - DR 92549	YX073F	YXA - F
DR 92562	YX073F	YXA - F

Operating 'Pool'

958

Notes

a) Not to be confused with 'KFA' Container Flats, which are also numbered in the 92500 - 92579 range, albeit with GMC, RLA and AVON prefixes.

b) Originally built 1987 - 1988 by Arbel Fauvet, France.

c) Converted from Internationally Registered vehicles in the 33-70-4666 and 33-70-4746 series.

d) Converted 2001 - 2004 by Jarvis, York.

YXA - D	**Built**	**: See text**
No. DR 92503	**Location**	**: Newport station**
	(Richard A. Jones)	

YXA - E Built : See text
No. DR 92563 Location : Warrington Bank Quay
(Dave Mulligan)

YXA - F Built : See text
No. DR 92548 Location : Burton-on-Trent
(Gareth Bayer)

YXA - B	**Built**	**: 2000 by Windhoff**
No. DR 98010	**Location**	**: Stafford**
	(Martyn Read)	

YXA - B	**Built**	**: 2000 by Windhoff**
No. DR 98954	**Location**	**: Temple Mills**
	(Martyn Read)	

YXA - B 'Windhoff' OHL Multi Purpose Vehicle

Number Range

DR 97011 - DR 97014

Notes

Owned by Network Rail.

YXA - B 'Windhoff' Electrification Multi Purpose Vehicle

Number Range

DR 98003 DR 98004 DR 98009 DR 98010

Design Code

YX001F YX001K

Operating 'Pool'

8004

Notes

Owned by Network Rail.

YXA - B 'Windhoff' Multi Purpose Vehicle

Number Range

DR 98901 + DR 98951 to DR 98931 + DR98982

Design Code

DR 98901 - DR 98925	YX001A
DR 98951 - DR 98975	YX001B
DR 98926 - DR 98932	YX002C
DR 98976 - DR 98982	YX002D

Operating 'Pool'

8004

Notes

Owned by Network Rail.

YXA - B
Built : 2004 by Windhoff
No. : DR 97011 and DR 97012
Location : Singlewell (CTRL)
(Richard A. Jones)

YXA - B
Built : 1998 - 2000 by Windhoff
No. : DR 98955 + DR 98905
Location : Temple Mills
(Richard A. Jones)

YZA - A

Pandrol Jackson Stoneblower

Number Range	DR 80200 - DR 80212
Design Code	YZ001A / B / C
Operating 'Pool'	8011
Notes	Owned by Amey, Balfour Beatty, Fastline and Network Rail.

YZA - A

Harsco Switch & Crossing Stoneblower

Number Range	DR 80301 DR 80302 DR 80303
Design Code	YZ003A
Operating 'Pool'	8011
Notes	Owned by Balfour Beatty, Amey and Harsco Track Technologies, respectively.

YZA - C

Harsco Stoneblower

Number Range	DR 80213 - DR 80217
Design Code	YZ001D
Operating 'Pool'	8011
Notes	Owned by Amey, Balfour Beatty, Fastline.

YZA - A	**Built**	**: 1995 - 2000 by Pandrol Jackson**
No. DR 80205	**Location**	**: Exeter St. Davids**
	(Martyn Read)	

YZA - A	**Built**	**: 2004 - 2005 by Harsco Track Technologies**
No. DR 80301	**Location**	**: Stratford**
	(Michael Groom)	

YZA - C	**Built**	**: 2004 by Harsco Track Technologies**
No. DR 80214	**Location**	**: Stratford**
	(Michael Groom)	

ZAA - U 2-axle Open Wagon - 'Pike'

Number Range

460051 460052

Design Code

ZA015A

Operating 'Pool'

8852 8854

Notes

Originally, several designs & livery were in this category.

Converted from OAA / OBA / OCA / VAA / VBA / VDA / SPA wagons.

Original wagons built 1969 - 1981 by BREL Ashford and Shildon.

ZAA - U	Built : See text
No. 460051	Location : Carlisle Citadel
	(Nathan Williamson)

ZCA 2-axle Open Wagon - 'Sea Urchin'

Suffix	Number Range	Design Code	Operating 'Pool'		
O	100001 - 100093	ZC019A	6292		
P	110000 - 110800	ZC011A to ZC011G	4123	6105	
			6292	9001	
		ZC012A to ZC012G	6105	6292	
			6816	9001	
B	200255 - 200322	ZC018A	4123	6292	
C	200326 - 200546	ZC020E / F	4123	6292	
B	200552 - 200647	ZC015A	4123	6292	
D	200655 - 200979	ZC014A	4123	6105	6292
D	210101 - 210398	ZC014A	4123	6105	6292
Q	460006 - 461094	ZC014A	4123	6105	6292
S	460769	ZC010A	6292		

Build / Conversion Notes:

Converted from OAA / OBA / OCA / VAA / VBA / VDA / SPA wagons.

Original wagons built 1969 - 1981 by BREL Ashford and Shildon.

Notes

As a result of conversions, there are several design variations & livery in all the above categories.

Some wagons in the above number ranges are prefixed by the letter DC, M or T.

Wagons in the ZCA - Q and ZCA - S categories were once classified as 'Sea Hare'.

ZCA - D	Built : See text
No. 210378	Location : Newport, ADJ
	(Martin Buck)

ZCA - O	Built : See text
No. 100008	Location : Westbury
	(Martyn Read)

ZCA - P | Built : See text
No. 110191 | Location : Westbury
(Martyn Read)

ZCA - Q | Built : See text
No. 460016 | Location : Swindon
(Martin Buck)

ZIA - C	Built	: 1961 by Cowans Sheldon
No. ADRC 96709	Location	: Tees Yard
	(Gareth Bayer)	

ZIA - C	Built	: 1977 by Cowans Sheldon
No. ADRC 96714	Location	: Westbury
	(Nathan Williamson)	

ZIA - C Cowans Sheldon 75 tonne Diesel Hydraulic (ex-steam) Breakdown Crane

Number Range

ADRC 96709

Design Code

Z1011C

Operating 'Pool'

8611

Notes

Owned by Network Rail.

ZIA - C Cowans Sheldon 75 tonne Diesel Hydraulic (Telescopic) Breakdown Crane

Number Range

ADRC 96714

Design Code

ZI012C

Operating 'Pool'

8617

Notes

Owned by Network Rail.

ZIB - C Cowans Sheldon 75 tonne Diesel Hydraulic (Telescopic) Breakdown Crane

Number Range	Design Code	Operating 'Pool'
ADRC 96702	Z1011A	8623
ADRC 96710	ZI012A	8615
ADRC 96712	Z1012A	8601
ADRC 96713	ZI012A	8635
ADRC 96715	ZI012A	8603

Notes

Owned by Network Rail.

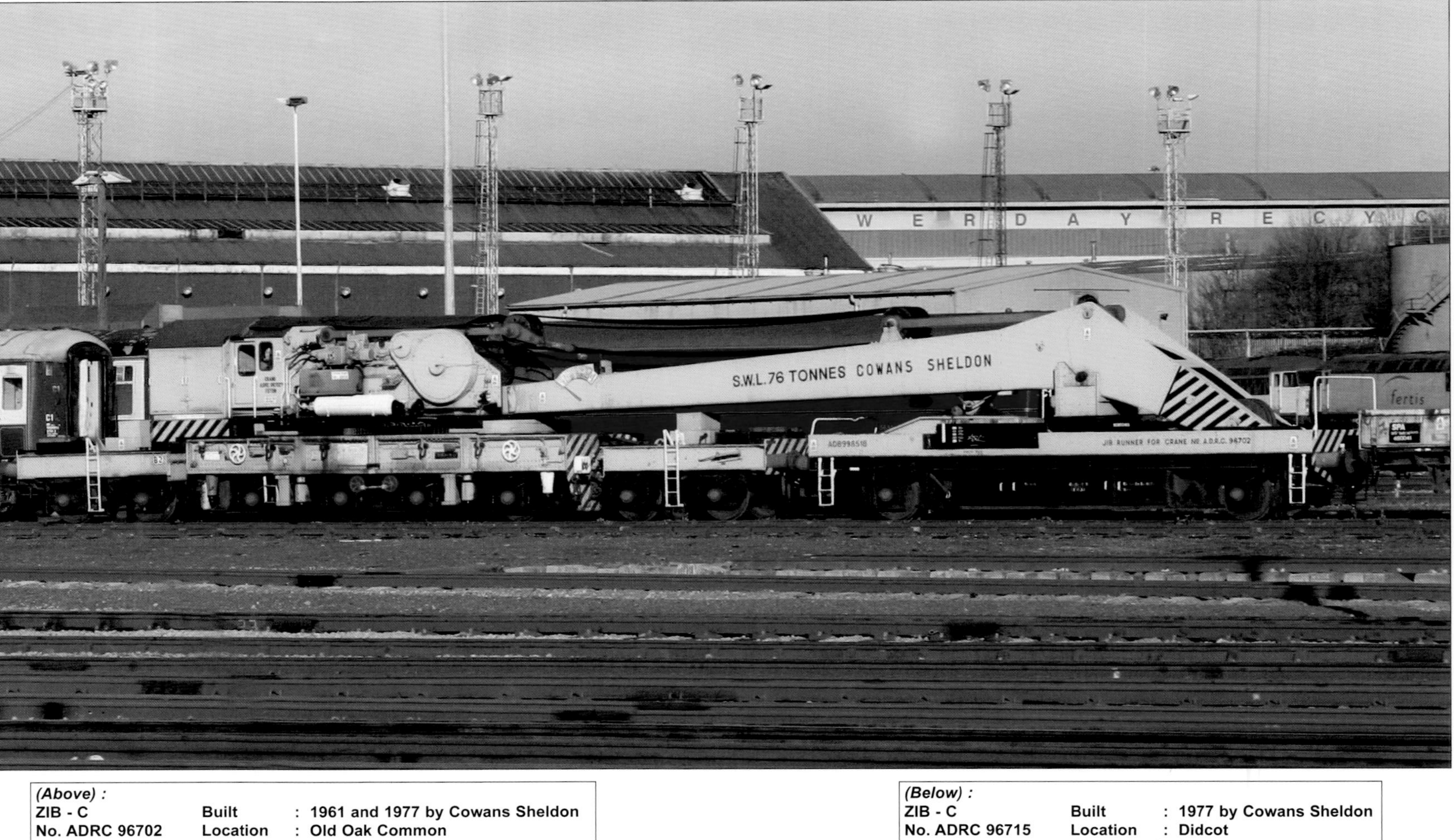

(Above) :
ZIB - C — Built : 1961 and 1977 by Cowans Sheldon
No. ADRC 96702 — Location : Old Oak Common
(Anthony Christie)

(Below) :
ZIB - C — Built : 1977 by Cowans Sheldon
No. ADRC 96715 — Location : Didcot
(Brian Daniels)

COWANS SHELDON
ADRC96715
S.W.L.75TONNES
RAILTRACK
RAILTRACK

ZOA - K — Kirow KRC810UK Heavy Duty Diesel Hydraulic Crane 100 tonne

Number Range	Design Code	Operating 'Pool'
DRK 81601	ZO063A	7350
DRK 81602	ZO063A	7104

Notes

DRK 61601 named *'Nigel Chester'*.

Built 2001.

Owned by GrantPlant.

ZOA - K — Kirow KRC1200UK Heavy Duty Diesel Hydraulic Crane 125 tonne

Number Range	Design Code	Operating 'Pool'
DRK 81611	ZO064A	7104
DRK 81612	ZO064A	7184
DRK 81613	ZO064A	7350

Notes

DRK 81611 named *'Malcolm L Pearce'*.

Built in 2004, 2005 and 2006, respectively.

Owned by Balfour Beatty, Colas Rail and GrantPlant, respectively.

ZOA - K — Kirow KRC250UK Heavy Duty Diesel Hydraulic Crane

Number Range	Design Code	Operating 'Pool'
DRK 81621	ZO066A	7350
DRK 81622	ZO066A	7350
DRK 81623	ZO067A	7096
DRK 81624	ZO067A	7096
DRK 81625	ZO067A	7096

Notes

Built 2006.

DRK 81621 & DRK 81622 owned by GrantPlant.

DRK 81623 - DRK 81624 owned by First Swietlesky.

(Opposite) :
ZOA - K — **Built : 2001 by Kirow**
No. DRK 81601 — **Location : Plymouth**
(Allan Wright)

GrantPlant
KIROW
GrantPlant
DRK 81601
Nigel Chester
Crane swings - keep clear

ZOA - K	Built	: 2004 by Kirow
No. DRK 81611	Location	: Lewington
	(Richard A. Jones)	

ZOA - K	Built	: 2006 by Kirow
No. DRK 81613	Location	: Carlisle Citadel
	(Nathan Williamson)	

ZOA - K	Built	: 2006 by Kirow
No. DRK 81621	Location	: Plymouth

(Allan Wright)

ZOA - K	Built	: 2004 by Kirow
No. DRK 81624	Location	: Plymouth

(Allan Wright)

ZOA - K Built : 2005 by Kirow
No. DRK 81612 Location : Carlisle Citadel
(Nathan Williamson)

ZUA - A 20t Ballast Brake Van- 'Shark'

Number Range	Design Code	Operating 'Pool'	Built	Lot No.
993715	ZU501U	6010	1956 by BRCW	2431
993718	ZU501U	6010	1956 by BRCW	2431
993738	ZU501U	6010	1956 by BRCW	2536
993777	ZU501S	6010	1956 by BRCW	2657
993826	ZU501U	6010	1956 - 1957 by BRCW	2931
993834	ZU501P	6010	1956 - 1957 by BRCW	2931
993842	ZU501P	6010	1956 - 1957 by BRCW	2931
993876	ZU501U	6010	1957 by BRCW	3040
993882	ZU501U	6010	1957 by BRCW	3040
993902	ZU501S	6010	1957 by BRCW	3040
993914	ZU501S	6010	1958 - 1959 by BRCW	3150
993922	ZU501T	6010	1962 by Central Wagon	3285

Illustrations:

(Above) :

ZUA - A	**Built : See text**	
No. 993922	**Location : Peterborough**	***(Gareth Bayer)***

Overleaf:

(Page 76) :

ZUA - A	**Built : See text**	
No. 993834	**Location : Hinksey Yard, Oxford**	***(Brian Daniels)***

(Page 77) :

ZUA - A	**Built : See text**	
No. 993876	**Location : Hinksey Yard, Oxford**	***(Brian Daniels)***

RACK
ATTENTION
THE LOAD MUST BE UNIFORMLY
DISTRIBUTED THROUGHOUT ALL HOPPERS
NOTICE
MUST ONLY BE MOVED
WITH DOORS CLOSED AND LOCKED
SHARK
ZUA
TARE 20 500KG
DB 993834
BRAKE-FORCE-9
carillion
www.carillionrail.com

SHARK
ZUA
TARE 19·35T
DB 993876
BRAKE FORCE 9 TON
A2

ZWA - E P & T DTS 62-N

Number Range

DR 72201 - DR 72214

Design Code

ZW998A

Operating 'Pool'

7073

7102

7160

7214

7460

Notes

These machines in this category are owned by either Balfour Beatty or Fastline.

ZWA - E	Built	: 1987 - 1988 by Plasser & Theurer
No. DR 72214	Location	: Peterborough
	(Gareth Bayer)	

ZWA - M — P & T 09-16 CSM

Number Range	DR 73001
Design Code	ZW997F
Operating 'Pool'	7882
Notes	This machine has an integrated trailer and is owned by Fastline.

ZWA - M — P & T 09-32 CSM

Number Range	DR 73101 - DR 73107
Design Code	ZW997G
Operating 'Pool'	7182 7262 7460
Notes	These machines have an integrated trailer. Owned by Colas Rail and Fastline.

ZWA - B — P & T 09-32-RT

Number Range	DR 73108
Design Code	ZW997E
Operating 'Pool'	7262
Notes	Owned by Amey and named *'Tiger'.*

ZWA - G — P & T 09-3X-RT

Number Range	DR 73109 DR 73110
Design Code	ZW001A
Operating 'Pool'	7160
Notes	DR 73110 named *'Peter White'.* Owned by Fastline.

ZWA - G — P & T 09-3X

Number Range	DR 73111 - DR 73118
Design Code	ZW001B / C
Operating 'Pool'	8009
Notes	DR 73111 named *'Reading Panel 1965 - 2005'.* Owned by Network Rail.

ZWA - M	Built	: 1987 by Plasser & Theurer
No. DR 73001	Location	: Water Orton
	(Richard A. Jones)	

ZWA - M	Built	: 1988 by Plasser & Theurer
No. DR 73101	Location	: Peterborough
	(Richard A. Jones)	

ZWA - B	Built	: 1988 by Plasser & Theurer
No. DR 73108	Location	: Bristol Temple Meads
	(Martyn Read)	

ZWA - G	Built	: 2000 - 2001 by Plasser & Theurer
No. DR 73109	Location	: Millmeece
	(Vince - OnTrackPlant)	

ZWA - G Built : 1988 - 2007 by Plasser & Theurer
No. DR 73112 Location : Reading West Yard *(Martyn Read)*

ZWA - E	Built	: 1974 - 1978 by Plasser & Theurer
No. DR 73246	Location	: March *(Gareth Bayer)*

ZWA - E P & T 07-16 Universal

Number Range

DR 73216 - DR 73278

Design Code

ZW312A / F / G / H / J

ZW328B / C

Operating 'Pool'

7102 7182 7460 7762 7880 7882

Notes

DR 73238 named *'Brian Langley'* / DR 73270 *'Allan Chamberlain'.*

These machines are owned by Balfour Beatty and Fastline.

ZWA - E P & T 07-275 Switch & Crossing

Number Range

DR 73307 - DR 73316

Design Code

ZW329C / D / E / F

Operating 'Pool'

7073 7102 7160 7880

Notes

DR 73311 named *'Cyril Dryland'.*

These machines are owned by Balfour Beatty and Fastline.

ZWA - M P & T 07-275 Switch & Crossing

Number Range

DR 73317 DR 73318 DR 73321

Design Code

ZW329G / H

Operating 'Pool'

7102 7182 7882

Notes

DR 73318 named *''Peter Atkinson'.*

These machines have an integrated trailer.

No. DR 73118 is owned by Balfour Beatty, the other two by Fastline.

ZWA - E	Built	: 1974 - 1978 by Plasser & Theurer
No. DR 73248	Location	: Bescot
	(Martyn Read)	

ZWA - E	Built	: 1978 - 1984 by Plasser & Theurer
No. DR 73309	Location	: Milford Junction
	(Richard A. Jones)	

ZWA - M Built : 1978 - 1984 by Plasser & Theurer
No. DR 73321 Location : Peterborough
(Gareth Bayer)

ZWA - E Built : 1977 - 1978 by Plasser & Theurer
No. DR 73435 Location : Peterborough
(Gareth Bayer)

ZWA - E P & T 07-32 Duomatic

Number Range	Design Code	Operating 'Pool'			
DR 73403	ZW330B	7880			
DR 73416 - DR 73435	ZW312K	7073	7160	7182	7460

Notes

All owned by Fastline, except Nos. DR 74424 and DR 73434 which are owned by Balfour Beatty.

ZWA - B P & T 07-32 Duomatic

Number Range

DR 73601

Design Code

ZW3312M

Operating 'Pool'

7460

Notes

Owned by Fastline.

ZWA - B	Built	: 1978 by Plasser & Theurer
No. DR 73601	Location	: Ditton
	(Richard A. Jones)	

ZWA - B P & T 08-32U-RT

Number Range

DR 73803 *'Alexander Graham Bell'*

Design Code

ZW340B

Operating 'Pool'

7000

Notes

Owned by Babcock Rail.

ZWA - B P & T 08-16U-RT

Number Range

DR 73804 *'James Watt'*

Design Code

ZW340B

Operating 'Pool'

7000

Notes

Owned by Babcock Rail.

ZWA - B P & T 08-16 / 32U-RT

Number Range

DR 73805 DR73806 *'Karine'*

Design Code

ZW340B

Operating 'Pool'

7370

Notes

Owned by Colas Rail.

ZWA - B | Built : 2002 by Plasser & Theurer
No. DR 73803 | Location : Craigo
(Jim Ramsay)

ZWA - B | Built : 2002 by Plasser & Theurer
No. DR 73805 | Location : Dawlish Warren
(Martyn Read)

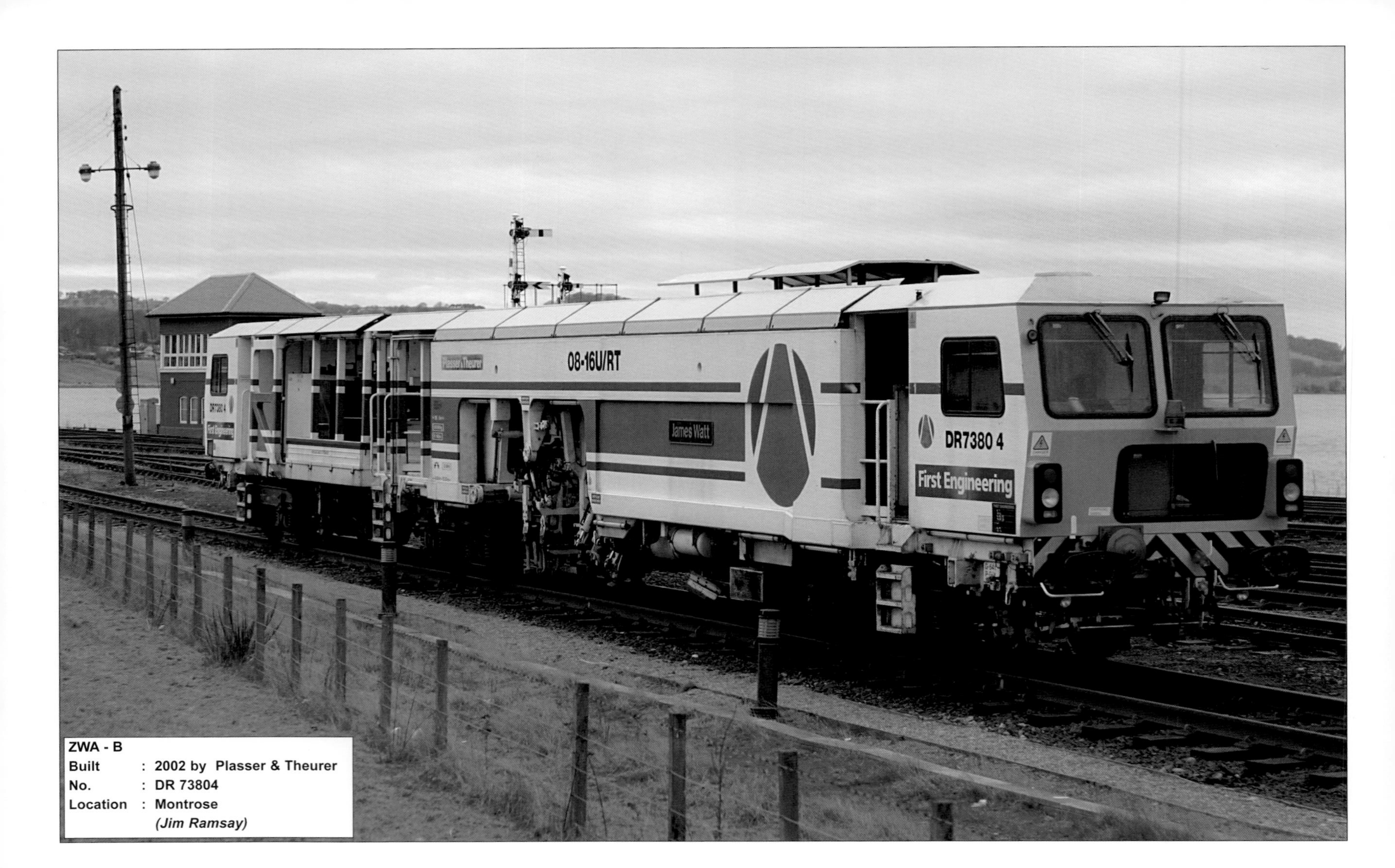

ZWA - B
Built : 2002 by Plasser & Theurer
No. : DR 73804
Location : Montrose
(Jim Ramsay)

ZWA - B | Built : See text
No.DR 73940 | Location : Peterborough
(Gareth Bayer)

ZWA - M P & T 08-275 Switch & Crossing

Number Range

DR 73901 DR 73902 DR 73903 *'George Mullineux'*

Design Code

ZW997C

Operating 'Pool'

7160 7182 7880

Notes

These machines have an integrated trailer.
No. DR 73901 is owned by Colas Rail, the other two by Fastline.

ZWA - B P & T 08-4x4 / 4S-RT

Number Range

DR 73904 *'Thomas Telford'*		DR 73905 *'Eddie King'*	
DR 73906	*DR 73907*	*DR 73908*	
DR 73909 *'Saturn'*		DR 73910 *'Jupiter'*	
DR 73914 *'Robert McAlpine'*		DR 73917	DR 73918
DR 73923 *'Mercury'*		DR 73929	
DR 73930	DR 73932	DR 73935	DR 73936
DR 73940	DR 73941	DR 73942	

Design Code

ZW348A / C / D / E / H / J / K / L

Operating 'Pool'

7000 7102 7160 7182 7190 7262 7274 7880

Notes

The machines in this category, built by Plasser & Theurer, are owned by:
Amey, Babcok Rail, Balfour Beatty, Colas Rail and Fastline.

Build Details:

1997 - 1999	:	DR 73904 - DR 73910
2000	:	DR 73914 - DR 73918
2001	:	DR 73923
2003	:	DR 73929 - DR 73936
2004	:	DR 73940 - DR 73942

Illustrations opposite:

(Top Right) :
ZWA - M **Built : 1987 - 1988 by Plasser & Theurer**
No. DR 73901 **Location : Carlisle Citadel station** ***(Richard Spray)***

(Bottom Right) :
ZWA - B **Built : See text**
No. DR 73909 **Location : Westbury station** ***(Martyn Read)***

Carlisle
73901
Carlisle
73901

73909

ZWA - B
No. DR 73918

Built : See text
Location : Norwich
(Gareth Bayer)

ZWA - K Built : 2000 by Plasser & Theurer
No. DR 73912 Location : Exeter St Davids station
(Martyn Read)

ZWA - K P & T 08-16 / 4x4C-RT

Number Range

DR 73911 *'Puma'*

DR 73912 *'Lynx'*

DR 73915 *'William Arrol"*

DR 73916 *'First Engineering'*

Design Code

ZW348D

Operating 'Pool'

7262

Notes

DR 73911 and DR 73912 owned by Amey.

DR 73915 and DR 73916 owned by Babcock Rail.

ZWA - B P & T 08-12 / 4x4C-RT

Number Range

DR 73913

Design Code

ZW348G

Operating 'Pool'

7102 7190 7274

Notes

Owned by Colas Rail.

Illustrations opposite:

(Top Right):

ZWA - K	**Built**	**: 2000 by Plasser & Theurer**	
No. DR 73915	**Location**	**: Hellifield**	***(Richard A. Jones)***

(Bottom Right):

ZWA - B	**Built**	**: 2000 by Plasser & Theurer**	
No. DR 73913	**Location**	**: Ely**	***(Gareth Bayer)***

First Engineering
Warning siren

AMEC
Warning siren
DR 73913

ZWA - B

P & T 08-16 / 4x4C100-RT

Number Range DR 73919 DR 73933 DR 73934

Design Code ZW348J

Operating 'Pool' 7000 7274

Notes These machines have an integrated trailer.
Owned by Babcock Rail and Colas Rail.

ZWA - K

P & T 08-16 / 4x4C80-RT

Number Range DR 73920 DR 73921 DR 73922 *'John Snowdon'*

Design Code ZW348D / G

Operating 'Pool' 7262

Notes Owned by Amey.

ZWA - E

P & T 08-4x4 / C100-RT

Number Range
DR 73924 'Atlas'
DR 73925 'Europa'
DR 73926 ' Stephen Keith Blanchard'
DR 73927 DR 73928
DR 73931
DR 73937 - DR 73939
DR 73943 DR 73944 DR 73945

Design Code ZW348H

Operating 'Pool' 7102 7190 7274

Notes These machines are owned by Balfour Beatty and Colas Rail.

ZWA - B

P & T Euromat 08-4x4S

Number Range DR 73946

Design Code ZW348K

Notes This machine is owned by Volker Rail, Holland.

ZWA - K	Built	: 2001 by Plasser & Theurer
No. DR 73921	Location	: Banbury
	(Martin Buck)	

ZWA - E	Built	: 2002 by Plasser & Theurer
No. DR 73924	Location	: Chester
	(Richard Spray)	

ZWA - B Built : 2003 by Plasser & Theurer
No.DR 73934 Location : Arbroath
(Jim Ramsay)

ZWA - B
No.DR 73946

Built : 2007 by Plasser & Theurer
Location : Willesden Junction
(Martyn Read)

ZWA - E Matisa B45 UE

Number Range

DR 75301 - DR 75303

Design Code

ZW352A

Operating 'Pool'

7350

Notes

Owned by GrantPlant.

ZWA - E **Built : 2000 by Matisa**
No. DR 75303 **Location : Doncaster**
(Mark Franklin)

ZWA - E Matisa B41 UE

Number Range

DR 75401 - DR 75407

Design Code

ZW353A

Operating 'Pool'

7350

Notes

These machines are owned by Balfour Beatty, Colas Rail and GrantPlant.

No. DR 75404 is fitted with PALAS equipment.

ZWA - E	Built	: 2003 - 2006 by Plasser & Theurer
No. DR 75401	Location	: Loughborough
	(Gareth Bayer)	

ZWA - E	Built	: 2003 - 2006 by Plasser & Theurer
No. DR 75406	Location	: Fairwood Junction, Westbury
	(Martin Buck)	

ZWA - D — Kershaw High Output

Number Range	DR 76101
Design Code	ZW337B
Operating 'Pool'	8850
Notes	Included for its unique design - scrapped.

ZWA - F — P & T RM95RT

Number Range	DR 76323	DR 76324
Design Code	ZW602A	
Operating 'Pool'	8008	
Notes	Network Rail machine / Operated by Fastline / Used with the MOBC train.	

ZWA - Y — P & T RM900T

Number Range	DR 76501	DR 76502
Design Code	ZW603A	
Operating 'Pool'	8009	
Notes	Network Rail machines / Operated by First Swietelsky / Used with HOBC.	

ZWA - V — P & T RM90RT

Number Range	DR 76601 *'Olwen'*
Design Code	ZW603A
Operating 'Pool'	8009
Notes	Owned by Colas Rail.

ZWA - Y
No. DR 76501

Built : 2004 & 2005 by Plasser & Theurer
Location : Fairwater Yard, Taunton

(Nathan Williamson)

Above / Below:

ZWA - F	**Built**	**: 2000 & 2001 by Plasser & Theurer**
No. DR 76324	**Location**	**: Paddock Wood**
	(Steve Hatcher - 2)	

ZWA - D Built : 1993 by Kershaw No. DR 76101 Forders Sidings *(Mark Franklin)*

ZWA - V   Built : 2006 by Plasser & Theurer   No. DR 76601   Eastleigh Works   *(Gareth Bayer)*

ZWA - K	Built	: 2005 by Matisa
No. DR 77802	Location	: Peterborough station
	(Martyn Read)	

ZWA - O	Built	: 2003 - 2007 by Plasser & Theurer
No. DR 77903	Location	: Fairwood Junction, Westbury
	(Martin Buck)	

ZWA - Z — AFM 2000 RT Track Finishing Machine

Number Range	DR 77001 DR 77002
Design Code	ZW100A
Operating 'Pool'	7000
Notes	This machine is ostensibly a 'longer' Ballast Regulator, similar to the ZWA detailed below (DR 77901 - DR 77905), which performs ballast ploughing & sweeping, plus dynamic track stabilisation. It also has a large hopper to carry ballast. Owned by First Swietelsky.

ZWA - K — USP 5000C

Number Range	DR 77306 - DR 77336
Design Code	ZW314E / G / H / J / K / L / M / N / P / T / U / V / W / X
Operating 'Pool'	7073 7102 7160 7180 7182 7460 7880 7882
Notes	Owned by Balfour Beatty, Colas Rail and Fastline.

ZWA - K — Matisa R24 S

Number Range	DR 77801 DR77802
Design Code	ZW351A
Operating 'Pool'	7350
Notes	Owned by GrantPlant.

ZWA - O — P & T USP 5000 RT

Number Range	DR 77901 - DR77905
Design Code	ZW314Q / R / S
Operating 'Pool'	7182 7274 8009
Notes	No. DR 77903 named *'Frank Jones'*. All machines owned by Network Rail, except No. DR 77901 owned by Colas Rail.

ZWA - Z
Built : 2006 by Plasser & Theurer
No : DR 77001
Location : Cambridge Sidings, Bletchley
(Richard A. Jones)

ZWA - K
Built : 1974 - 1986 by Plasser & Theurer
No. : DR 77328
Location : Bescot
(Gareth Bayer)

ZWA - N — Loram Schweerbau SPML 15

Number Range	DR 79200
Design Code	ZW600A
Operating 'Pool'	1204
Notes	Owned by Loram.

ZWA - X — Loram Schweerbau SPML 17

Number Range	DR 79201
Design Code	ZW601A
Operating 'Pool'	1204
Notes	Owned by Loram.

ZWA - S
ZWA - T — Speno RPS 32-2

Number Range DR 79221 - DR 79226

Train Set Formation Details

Number	Carkind / Design Code		Operating 'Pool'
DR 79221	ZWA - S	ZW002A	1280
DR 79222 - DR 79225	ZWA - T	ZW002B / C / C / D	1280
DR 79226	ZWA - S	ZW002E	1280

Notes Owned by Speno.

(Above)	ZWA - S				
Built	: 1990 by Speno	No. DR 79221	Location	: Ruddington - GCR	*(Vince - OnTrackPlant)*
(Opposite)	ZWA - X				
Built	: 2000 by Loram	No. DR 79201	Location	: Appleby-in-Westmorland	*(Roy Hennefer)*
(Below)	ZWA - T				
Built	: 1990 by Speno	No. DR 79225	Location	: Ruddington - GCR	*(Vince - OnTrackPlant)*

ZWA - N
No. DR 79200

Built : 1993 by Loram
Location : Dundee
(Jim Ramsay)

ZWA - L
Built : 2003 by Harsco Track Technologies
No : DR 79273 + DR 79263
Location : Cardiff Central station
(Richard A. Jones)

ZWA - L Loram C21

Train Set C21 (01)

Number Range	DR 79231 - DR 79237
Design Code	ZW003A / F / B / E / B / B / D, respectively.
Operating 'Pool'	1250
Notes	Owned by Loram.

Train Set C21 (02)

Number Range	DR 79241 - DR 79247
Design Code	ZW004A / B / C / D / E / F / G, respectively.
Operating 'Pool'	8772
Notes	Owned by Network Rail.

Train Set C21 (03)

Number Range	DR 79251 - DR 79257
Design Code	ZW004A / B / C / D / E / F / G, respectively
Operating 'Pool'	8774
Notes	Owned by Network Rail.

Loram C21 Formation Details

Each Loram train set comprises 7 vehicles with 64 grinding stones in total with an identical formation for sets C21 (01), (02) and (03), albeit with different numbers.

For example:

No.	**Purpose**
DR 79231	Control vehicle with driving cab.
DR 79232	Fluid vehicle with under-slung water tank.
DR 79233 / 4 / 5 / 6	Grinding vehicles, each with 16 grinding stones, dust extraction system and pwer unit.
DR 79237	Control vehicle with driving cab.

ZWA - H Harsco Track Technologies RGH Switch & Crossing 20C

Number Range	DR 79261 + DR 79271 - DR79265 + DR 79275
Design Code	ZW005A / B
Operating 'Pool'	8770
Notes	This rail grinder comprises two separate vehicles, DR 7926x + DR 7927x. Owned by Network Rail.

ZWA - L
Built : 1995 - 2003 by Loram
No. : Loram C2103 train set
Location : Wandsworth Road
(Martyn Read)

ZWA — Eiv de Brieve DU94BA TRAMM with Crane

Number Range DR 97001

Notes Owned by Network Rail (CTRL).

Ex-SNCF.

ZWA - Q — P & T GP-TRAMM with Trailer

Number Range DR 98204 - DR 98220

Design Code ZW999C / D / E / L / R

Operating 'Pool' 7073 7102 7262

Notes All have 'A' and 'B' ends.

Owned by Amey, Balfour Beatty and Fastline.

ZWA - Q — Geismar GP-TRAMM with Trailer

Number Range DR 98303

Design Code ZW999N

Notes Owned by Dartmoor Railway.

ZWA - Q — Geismar GP-TRAMM VMT 860 PL / UM with Trailer

Number Range DR 98307 DR 98308

Design Code ZW999J

Operating 'Pool' 7274

Notes Owned by Colas Rail.

ZWA
No. DR 97001

Built : 2003 by Eiv de Brieve
Location : Dollands Moor
(Steve Hatcher)

ZWA - Q
No. DR 98220

Built : 1984 - 1988 by Plasser & Theurer
Location : Yeovil Junction
(Martyn Read)

ZWA - Q
No. DR 98303

Built : 1985 by Geismar
Location : Meldon Quarry
(Richard A. Jones)

ZWA - Q — Built : 1985 by Geismar
No. DR 98308 — Location : Eastleigh
(Martyn Read)

ZWA - J Beilhack Self Propelled Rotary Snowblower

Number Range	Design Code	Operating 'Pool'
ADB 968500	ZW331A	8111
ADB 968501	ZW335A	8109

Notes

Owned by Network Rail and based at Motherwell.

ZWA	**Built**	**: 1978 - 1983 by Plasser & Theurer**
No. ADB 968500	**Location**	**: Motherwell**
	(Dave Hunt)	

OPPOSITE:
(Top Right)

ZWB - A	**Built**	**: 1978 - 1983 by Plasser & Theurer**	
No. DR 76304	**Location**	**: Toton**	***(Gareth Bayer)***

(Bottom Right)

ZWB - A	**Built**	**: 1978 - 1983 by Plasser & Theurer**	
No. DR 76315	**Location**	**: Rugby**	***(Martyn Read)***
(now withdrawn)			

ZWB - A P & T RM74

Number Range

DR 76300 - DR 76322

Design Code

ZW307H

Operating 'Pool'

7426 7880

Notes

Owned by Fastline - except No. DR 76313 owned by Bahna Engineer.

ZWQ- B — P & T 08-16 / 90

Number Range	DR 73502	DR 73503
Design Code	ZW997H	ZW344B
Operating 'Pool'	7102	7460
Notes	Owned by Balfour Beatty.	

ZWQ- B — P & T 08-16 / 90-275 Switch & Crossing

Number Range	DR 75201	DR 75202
Design Code	ZW996A	
Operating 'Pool'	7102	
Notes	Owned by Balfour Beatty.	

ZWY - B — P & T 08-275 ZW Switch & Crossing

Number Range	DR 75204
Design Code	ZW350B
Operating 'Pool'	7460
Notes	Owned by Trackwork.

ZWQ - B	Built	: 1988by Plasser & Theurer
No. DR 73502	Location	: Bedford
	(Gareth Bayer)	

ZWQ - B	Built	: 1991 by Plasser & Theurer
No. DR 75201	Location	: Ashford
	(Steve Hatcher)	

ZWY - B	Built	: 1991 by Plasser & Theurer
No. DR 75204	Location	: Kirk Sandall
	(Roy Hennefer)	

ZXQ - R Structure Gauging Train 'Optical Car'

Number Range

460000

Design Code

YX147D

Operating 'Pool'

8910

ZXQ - R	Built	: 1977 by BREL Ashford
No. DC 460000	Location	: Bristol Temple Meads
	(Nathan Williamson)	

ZZA - B Independent Drift Plough

Number Range	ADB 965203 - ADB 965243
Design Code	ZZ501B
Operating 'Pool'	8103 8105 8107 8115 8135 8137 8139 8191 8193
Notes	Owned by Network Rail - based at:

Bristol (2)	Carlisle (2)	Doncaster (2)	Inverness (2)
Margam (2)	Mossend (4)	Peterborough (2)	Thornaby (2)
Tonbridge (2)	Wigan (2)		

ZZA - S Beilhack Type PB600 Plough

Number Range	ADB 965576 - ADB 965581 ADB 966096 - ADB 966099
Design Code	ZZ503A ZZ504A
Operating 'Pool'	8101 8117 8121 8151 8189
Notes	Fitted on Class 40 Bogies.
	Owned by Network Rail - based at:

Carlisle (2)	Doncaster (2)	Mossend ((2)	Peterborough (2)
Wigan (2)			

ZZA - B No. ADB 965210 Location : Tonbridge West Yard
(Richard A. Jones)

ZZA - S No. ADB 965578 Location : Temple Mills
(Steve Hatcher)

ZZA - S No. ADB 966098 Location : Peterborough
(Martyn Read)

(Opposite):
ZWA - K Built : 1974 - 1986 by Plasser & Theurer
No. DR 77313 Location : York *(Martyn Read)*

Glossary

Carkinds Removed

Since compilation of 'Wagon Recognition - Volume 2' commenced in April 2008, some wagon types along with some OTP machines have been stored or withdrawn altogether. Some of these are detailed below along with an image of each for completeness.

YDA	**Starfer Single Line Spoil Handling System Wagon**
Number Range	DR 92201 - DR 92212
Design Code	YD002A
Operating 'Pool'	8856

YJA	**Harsco Track Technology P-811S Track Renewal Train**
Number Range	DR 78901
Design Code	YR501A
Operating 'Pool'	7898

YRA	**Stores Van**
Number Range	889400 (Ex-Danzas 33. 70. 2797 021)
Design Code	YR501E
Operating 'Pool'	7898
Notes	Built 1979 by BREL Shildon and converted 1991 by Jarvis, York.

YTX / YTW*	***'Queen Mary'* Bogie Brake Van**
Number Range	ADS 56299 KDS 56305*
Design Code	YT500
Notes	Pre-Nationalisation, ex-Southern Region, bogie brake van.

YVA	**Cable Drum Carrier**
Number range	KDC 950034 - KDC 950849
Design Code	YV078A / B / C / D
Operating 'Pool'	6892 6912
Notes	Numbered within BDA / BEA / BFA 950001 - 951249 number range. Built and modified in various 'Lots' between 1975 - 1981 at BREL Ashford, Shildon and Swindon.

YZA	**Wet Spot Treatment Machine**
Number Range	DR 76401
Design Code	YZ002B
Operating 'Pool'	7274
Notes	Prototype stoneblower. Built by Plasser & Theurer 1984 / Re-built 1999.

ZBA — 2-Axle Open Ballast Wagon - 'Rudd'

Number Range 972029 - 972796
Design Code ZB001A ZB002A ZB003A
Operating 'Pool' 6994 7106
Notes Converted 1989 - 1991 by Marcroft and CC Crump Ltd.

ZDA — 2-Axle Open Ballast Wagon - 'Bass'

Number Range 110000 - 110800 112000 - 112399 210101 - 210398
Notes Some numbers prefixed BDC, DC, M or T.
Converted from OAA / OBA / OCA / VAA / VBA / VDA / SPA wagons.
Original wagons built 1969 - 1981 by BREL Ashford and Shildon.

ZSB — Tunnel Ventilation Unit

Number Range ADE 901720
Design Code ZS507C
Operating 'Pool' 7106

ZWA — Cowans Sheldon BRM 1000

Number Range DR 77401 DR 77402
Design Code ZW994C
Operating 'Pool' 7460

YDA
No. DR 92210
Built : by Starfer
Location : York
(Martyn Read)

DC 79801 *(i)*

DC 79801 *(ii)*

DC 79801 *(iii)*

(Above / Below / Opposite) :

YJA	**Built**	**: 2004 by Harsco Track Technologies**
No. DC 79801	**Location**	**: Didcot Yard**
	(Brian Daniels (5))	

DC 79801 *(iv)*

YRA	Built	: Built 1979 / Converted 1991
No. 889400	Location	: Didcot
	(Brian Daniels)	

YTW	Built	: 1936 by Lancing Works
No. KDS 56305	Location	: Newton Abbot
	(Nathan Williamson)	

YVA	Built	: See text
No. KDC 950849	Location	: Didcot Yard
	(Brian Daniels)	

YZA	Built	: See text
No. DR 76401	Location	: Woking
	(Steve Hatcher)	

ZBA	Built	: See text
No. 972068	Location	: London Bridge Station
	(Martyn Read)	

ZDA	Built	: See text
No. 110090	Location	: Parkeston Quay, Harwich
	(Gareth Bayer)	

ZSB **Built : 1940**
No. ADE 901720 **Location : Toton Yard**
(Richard A. Jones)

ZWA **Built : 1984 by Cowans Sheldon**
No. DR 77401 **Location : Truro**
(Martyn Read)

'OTP' EXPLAINED

This a brief summary of the functions performed by the OTP previously illustrated.

Ballast Cleaners (ZWA)

A ballast cleaner is a machine that specialises in cleaning railway track ballast.

Over a period of time, ballast becomes worn down and rounded, which hinders the tessellation of pieces of ballast with one another, thus reducing effectiveness. Combined with water, fine pieces of granite stick together, making it like a solid lump of concrete, hindering track drainage and so reducing the flexibility of the ballast to constrain the track as it moves under traffic.

Therefore, ballast cleaning is undertaken to remove this ballast, screen it and replace the worn ballast with fresh ballast. A ballast cleaner has a cutter bar running beneath sleeper level excavating all of the ballast under the sleepers to a specified depth. A conveyor then moves the ballast up into the ballast cleaner, where it passes through a mesh. Those pieces smaller than the mesh size fall through and are rejected; those bigger than the mesh are returned to the track along with fresh ballast.

Ballast Regulators (ZWA)

A ballast regulator is used to shape and distribute the ballast that supports the rail track and is often used in conjunction with Tampers. It has adjustable ploughs for working in the gauge and between adjacent tracks with a rotating brush (feeding a conveyor), which moves any surplus ballast out of the way, or into an internal hopper.

Unique machine No.77001 is a sort of ballast regulator, known as a 'Track Finishing Machine', performing ballast ploughing and sweeping along with dynamic track stabilisation. In addition, it has a large ballast hopper, which can hold 18 tonnes of ballast.

Ballast & Spoil Handling Trains (YDA)

There are a number of set-formation trains, which distribute ballast and other track laying aggregates, which basically fall into two main categories.

The first, and the only one of this design, is the DB Schenker 'Skako' Ballast Distribution Train, made up of ten wagons, each with a two-compartment hopper wagon, which distributes ballast from each hopper by way of a feeder onto a conveyor, thence the track.

The other train features the distinctive Plasser & Theurer High Output Ballast Cleaner (HOBC) formation, which works on the tracks' ballast foundation. The huge yellow machine (see illustration opposite) consists of 15 ballast hopper wagons, which use a swivel conveyor to distribute the ballast, plus interface / power wagon.

Whilst on site, this remarkable 'all-in-one' machine handles the following processes continuously:

- excavates ballast from beneath the track, while holding the track in position.
- passes the excavated material through large vibrating sieves and removes the unwanted 'fines' to specialist wagons in the train.
- returns the larger pieces of ballast back to the track.

(Above) : Typical formation of a Ballast & Spoil Handling Train (High Output Ballast Cleaner) comprising 15 YDA hoppers in the consist, seen during marshalling manoeuvres at Fairwater Yard, Taunton. *(Nathan Williamson)*

Dynamic Track Stabiliser (ZWA)

This particular type of track machine was developed in the 1970's by Plasser & Theurer. It is a self-propelled vehicle with eight retractable wheels under the machine, which are pressed down on the rails with considerable force. This enables the track to 'settle' on the ballast and means that no speed restrictions are needed following track work.

Rail Grinders (ZWA)

The purpose of these machines is to 'grind' the rail to fine tolerances using sets of grinding stones mounted beneath the machine, which are lowered on to the rail. This results in improved 'wheel to rail' interface and efficient running.

Serco operate five grinding machines - two Self Propelled Modular machines (SPML) and three C21 high-output machines, all built by Loram, USA:

SPML 15 : 32-stone, 3-unit permanently coupled formation.
SPML 17 : 16-stone, 3-unit permanently coupled formation.
C21 01/2/3 : 64-stone, 7-unit permanently coupled formation.

There is also the Speno RPS 32-2 rail grinding machine, which has 32-stones and is a permanently coupled 6-vehicle formation.

Harsco Track Technologies developed the self-propelled RGH 20C 10-stone grinding vehicle for use on switch & crossings and, as they operate in pairs, each formation provides 20-stones effectiveness.

MPVs - Multi-Purpose Vehicles (YXA / ZWA)

The Multiple-Purpose Vehicle (MPV) is a purpose-built departmental vehicle, built in Germany by Windhoff, based on the Windhoff "CargoSprinter" units operated by Deutsche Bahn (Germany) and CRT Group (Australia). The concept is that each vehicle has a driving cab, with under floor engine / transmission and Multiple Unit (MU) control, and a flat load bed that can carry a combination of modules.

There are several self-propelled vehicles in this category and, for ease of reference, a description is given according to number range:

The DR 970xx vehicles are used for maintenance on the Channel Tunnel Rail Link (CTRL) high speed lines, which carry a variety of modules for access to the overhead power lines, drain clearance, track inspection and weedspraying, for example.

The vehicles in the DR 980xx series are divided into two main categories - piling work and overhead line renewal. The piling vehicles also carry lifting equipment and undertake the erection of OLE support masts once piling is complete.

All vehicles in the DR 982xx and DR 983xx series are known as GP TRAMMs - 'General Purpose Track Repair and Maintenance Machine', built by either Geismar or Plasser & Theurer. The TRAMM consists of a main vehicle plus trailer, known as 'A' and 'B' ends, respectively, and can be towed or run under its own power.

These vehicles carry a crane / excavator and undertake a variety of uses, such as carrying rails to permanent way sites, ploughing ballast and positioning rails.

Finally, there are the DR 989xx MPVs, which consist of a 'Master' power driving unit (Nos. DR 98901 - DR 98925) plus a 'Slave' unpowered driving unit (DR 98951 - DR 98975). Each has a 50' platform to carry modules, ostensibly for autumn leaf-fall, third-rail de-icing and weed-killing operations.

Some of the latter MPVs have also been deployed on revenue-earning freight duties, such as conveying Bulmers produce to & from Hereford and on timber traffic (logs) on the Cambrian line from Aberystwyth.

Track Renewal Machines (YJA)

This is the Matisa P 95 UK Track Renewal Machine, which is made up of several vehicles:

Amenity & messing vehicle
Fastener cutting vehicle
Fastener Collection vehicle
Powered sleeper removal & insertion vehicle
Sleeper handling gantry
Sleeper handling vehicle
Workshop

This train removes sleeper fastenings, re-railing, removing old sleepers and replacing with new ones, working in conjunction with purpose-built YXA Sleeper Carrying Wagons. These YXAs are used to bring in the new steel & concrete sleepers and to take away the old timber or concrete sleepers.

Stoneblowers (YZA)

These machines measure track alignment with on-board computers determining lift, slew and the quantity of stones for each sleeper. The stoneblower will pneumatically inject (ie. 'blow') small stones under the sleeper to ensure the correct level of track.

Tampers (ZWA)

A ballast tamper or tamping machine is a machine used to pack (or tamp) the track ballast under railway tracks to make the tracks more durable - a task previously carried out by manual labour! These machines are efficient and labour-saving, which is just as well considering the widespread use of concrete sleepers which are too heavy (usually over 250 kg) to be packed into the ballast by hand.

Early machines only lifted track and packed ballast, while more modern machines (sometimes referred to as 'Tamper-liner') also correct the alignment of the rails to make them parallel and level, in order to achieve smooth running of passing trains.

Tamping machines come in a variety of shapes, sizes and technical specifications and for each rail there is a tamping unit attached to the main frame by means of vertical guide columns and a lifting / lowering hydraulic cylinder. The tamping unit consists of tamping tools (arms or "tines"), a vibration motor, a vibration shaft and flywheel. For each sleeper, a tamping unit is provided with four pairs of tamping arms: one each side of the sleeper - i.e. 16 tamping arms for tamping a single sleeper.

Some tampers have 32 arms to tamp two sleepers at a time and the 09-3X series has 48 arms. There are also 'Switch & Crossing' tampers, which are generally more powerful in order to deal with the weight of points and have a different layout of equipment.

WAGON & OTP 'POOL' CODES

All wagons and On Track Plant recorded in this book are allocated 'Pool Codes' on TOPS for means of identification, allocation and ownership. Here is a list of relevant 'Pool' Codes:

'Pool'	Owner	Description
0958	GE / Jarvis	Rail Recovery Train
1204	Railtest	Rail Grinder - Derby
1250	Schwebau	Loram Rail Grinder
6010	DBS	Ploughs
6105	DBS	ZCA Fleet
6107	DBS	Skako Train
6109	DBS	Seacows
6280	DBS	Seacows / Sealions
6282	DBS	Seacows / Sealions
6292	DBS	Stone & Spoil
6718	DBS	Flat Salmon - 60mph
6720	DBS	Flat Salmon
6722	DBS	Bolstered Salmon
6728	DBS	Bolstere Osprey
6816	DBS	OBA - Wooden Doors
6820	DBS	65' Borail for Switch & Crossing
6892	DBS	Cable Layers
6912	DBS	Cable Layers
6994	DBS	ZBA / ZCA for scrap
7073	Jarvis	Miscellaneous Rail Vehicles
7096	First Swietlesky	Kirow Cranes
7102	Balfour Beatty	On Track Machines
7104	Balfour Beatty	Cranes & Tracklayer
7106	Balfour Beatty	Unpowered Vehicles
7160	Jarvis	On Track Machines
7180	Carillion	On Track Machines
7182	Carillion	Ballast Machines
7184	Carillion	Kirow Crane Set
7190	Carillion	On Track Machines
7200	Jarvis	Ballast Cleaners
7214	Jarvis	Plant - Engineers
7222	Jarvis	Cranes - Booths
7262	Amey	On Track Machines
7274	Amec-Rail	On Track Machines
7350	Grant Rail	Track Machines & Wagons
7370	Seco / DCG	Ballast Tampers
7426	Jarvis	On Track Machines
7460	Jarvis	On Track Machines
7762	Jarvis	Plasser
7776	Jarvis	Tracklayer
7880	Jarvis	Plant - West
7882	Jarvis	Plant - East
7883	Jarvis	AC Foundations
7898	Jarvis	East Coast Renewal

'Pool'	Owner	Description
8002	Network Rail	Rail Head Treatment
8004	Network Rail	MPV'S
8006	Network Rail	Container Flats
8008	Network Rail	Ballast Cleaners
8009	Network Rail	On Track Plant
8011	Network Rail	Stoneblowers
8101	Network Rail	Snowploughs
8103	Network Rail	Snowploughs
8105	Network Rail	Snowploughs - Drift
8107	Network Rail	Snowploughs - Drift
8109	Network Rail	Rotary Snowblower
8111	Network Rail	Rotary Snowblower
8115	Network Rail	Snowploughs - Drift
8117	Network Rail	Snowplough - Beilhack
8121	Network Rail	Snowplough - Beilhack
8135	Network Rail	Snowploughs - Drift
8137	Network Rail	Snowploughs - Drift
8139	Network Rail	Snowploughs - Drift
8151	Network Rail	Snowplough - Beilhack
8189	Network Rail	Snowplough - Beilhack
8191	Network Rail	Snowploughs - Drift
8193	Network Rail	Snowploughs - Drift
8540	Network Rail	Sleeper Carriers
8601	Network Rail	Breakdown Train
8603	Network Rail	Breakdown Train
8611	Network Rail	Breakdown Train
8615	Network Rail	Breakdown Train
8617	Network Rail	Breakdown Train
8623	Network Rail	Breakdown Train
8635	Network Rail	Breakdown Train
8770	Network Rail	Harsco Rail Grinder
8772	Network Rail	Loram Rail Grinder
8774	Network Rail	Loram Rail Grinder
8810	Network Rail	Long Welded Train
8812	Network Rail	Long Welded Train
8814	Network Rail	Long Welded Train
8832	Network Rail	Rail Delivery Train
8834	Network Rail	Rail Delivery Train
8840	Network Rail	Train Relaying System
8844	Network Rail	Track Renewal Train
8850	Network Rail	High Output Ballast Distribution
8852	Network Rail	Ballast Distribution
8854	Network Rail	Spoil Handling
8858	Network Rail	Material Handling Train
8860	Network Rail	Ballast Cleaning
8910	Network Rail	Structure Gauging

BIBLIOGRAPHY

Recommended sources of reference:

Websites

garethbayer.co.uk (Wagons on the Web)	Gareth Bayer
wagons.fotopic.net	Nathan Williamson
ukrailways.fototopic.net	Martyn Read
briandaniels.fotopic.net	Brian Daniels
richardjones8646.fotopic.net	Richard A. Jones
ontrackplant.com	Ben & Vince

Books

Combined Wagon Datafile	Inter City Railway Society 192 Alvechurch Road West Heath Birmingham B31 3PW	No ISBN number
UK & Continental Wagons	AEB Rail Publications 27 Chatsworth Avenue Warton PRESTON PR4 1BQ	No ISBN number
On Track Plant	NPT Publishing 26 Priory Gardens Langstone NEWPORT NP18 2JG	ISBN 0-9537463-5-6